BOBBY AND MANDEE'S MONSTER TIPS FOR A HAPPY HALLOWEEN

ROBERT KAHN
&
BOB SWIFT

Illustrated by Daniel Majan

Copyright © 2020 by ROBERT KAHN. 804796

All rights reserved. No part of this book may
be reproduced or transmitted in any form
or by any means, electronic or mechanical,
including photocopying, recording, or by any
information storage and retrieval system, without
permission in writing from the copyright owner.

To order additional copies of this book, contact:
Xlibris
1-888-795-4274
www.Xlibris.com
Orders@Xlibris.com

ISBN: Softcover   978-1-7960-8668-3
         EBook   978-1-7960-8667-6

Print information available on the last page

Rev. date: 03/23/2020

BOBBY AND MANDEE'S MONSTER TIPS FOR A HAPPY HALLOWEEN

Hi Mandee, it's almost time to go Trick-or-Treating. Before we change into our costumes, let's go over the rules mom and dad taught us for being safe tonight.

What about your costume Mandee, what are some tips for it?

Bobby, since masks can limit or block your eyesight, you might consider makeup ⁻ and hats instead. If you wear a hat, make sure it won't slide over your eyes so you can see where you're going.

If you wear a mask, make sure that it fits properly and that there is plenty of airflow for breathing. Also, it shouldn't block your vision, so that you can see everything that is around you.

The costume should have reflective markings on it so that you are easily visible at night. Never have your name, address, or phone number written on the outside of the costume. Have your parents secure an identification tag somewhere inside the costume, where it can't be seen by people. This will prevent strangers from calling you by your name.

Make sure the material on the costume is fire resistant, and never wear a paper costume. Any accessories, like masks, beards, wigs, for the costume should also be fire resistant. Never use a paper or a cloth sack for your trick-or-treat bag. They can easily break or they can catch on fire. Mandee, fires and burns are the third leading cause of unintentional injury, or death, among children.

Remember, if your going to use a pirate's sword, knife, or a gun for the costume, they should be flexible so you can't get hurt. Also, make sure that it looks like a toy and not a real one. A real looking one might get you into trouble with other children, gangs, or even the police.

Bobby, I know the costume should fit well and be short enough so that you won't be tripping on it. Also, make sure that your shoes fit well and that they are comfortable. Remember we will be trick-or-treating after dark. Put reflective tape on your Trick-or-Treat plastic bucket, or bag that you use for candy. This is so others will be able to see you.

That was very good Mandee. Now how about the safety rules when you go Trick-or-Treating.

Ok Bobby, you should always eat dinner before you go Trick-or-Treating. This will stop you from getting hungry so you won't eat any of the candy before you have a trusted adult check that it hasn't been tampered with. Never go Trick-or-Treating by yourself. It is safer that everyone under 10 years old, or under, should go with their parents. This will also prevent bullies from scaring you and taking your candy.

If your 11 years old, or older, go with at least two other friends. It's just smart to go with others because if you get hurt, someone will be there to help you. Tonight is the night that you're coming in contact with strangers. Having others along is just being safe.

Always tell your parents where you're going to be Trick-or-Treating. With your parents, you should make a map of where you're going to be at. You should stay in your own neighborhood and have a specific time when you will return home. It is good to stay away from strangers, and their animals, while you are going from house to house.

Review the tips, with your parents, for calling 9-1-1. You may want to take a cell phone with you in case of an emergency, or if your parents need to call you.

For Trick-or-Treating after dark, always take a flashlight and keep it on so others can see you. You, or your parents, need to make sure there are new batteries in the flashlight so that it won't stop shining tonight. Remember, always use a flashlight, chemical light sticks, or a battery powered lantern for lighting. Never use a candle, or anything with a flame, for lighting your way.

When you're Trick-or-Treating, keep away from pumpkins, or other Halloween decorations, that have a candle lit in them. Children get hurt each year because part of their costume catches on fire. If this ever happens to you, or a friend your with, REMEMBER! STOP! DROP! AND ROLL! until the flame is out. Then call 9-1-1.

Mandee, tell me what to do once you leave your house. Ok Bobby, when you're Trick-or-Treating keep your flashlight on and walk on the sidewalks, not in the street. If there aren't any sidewalks, then you have to walk in the street. Stay at the farthest edge away from the traffic. This will keep a safe distance between you and the moving cars. Make sure you are walking so that you are facing the traffic. Remember to stay on well lit streets and walk everywhere, don't run because you may fall and get hurt.

Never cross the street by walking between parked cars. This is because the driver of the car can't see you. Also, don't crisscross back and forth across a street. Trick-or-Treat on one side of the street, then cross and Trick-or-Treat on the other side of the street. Don't take shortcuts by cutting across someone's yard and stay out of alleys.

Obey the traffic laws by crossing a street in the crosswalks. If there aren't crosswalks, cross at the street corners. If you are wearing a mask, which restricts your ability to see, remove it before you cross a street. Always look both ways for moving cars, before you cross. Remember to walk across the street, not run. This will give the cars time to see you, and stop.

Mandee, just because a car stops for you, another car may not see you. Make sure all cars are stopped before you cross a street on Halloween. Also remember, if a stranger in a car asks you something, just keep walking. You're not being rude, you are being safe. Strangers need to talk to adults, not children.

Ok Mandee, let's hear the tips when you're going to someone's house Trick-or-Treating.

Bobby, always stay with the friends you're Trick-or-Treating with; never wander off by yourself. You and your friends should always agree which house you're going to next, and go to each house together.

This is just being safe!

Trick-or-Treat at well-lighted houses. These are the houses where treats are being given at. Always "THANK" everyone who gives you a treat. This makes you a polite Trick-or-Treater. Be careful not to break or destroy anything that's on the property while you are there.

Sometimes a person in a car will offer you a treat. This is a trick bad strangers will use to get you into their car and take you with them. You're smart to ignore them and not get close to their car.

NEVER GET INTO A STRANGER'S CAR TO TAKE A TREAT!

Don't go into a house that you're Trick-or-Treating at if you and your parents don't know them well. Always accept the treat at the door. NEVER ENTER A STRANGER'S HOME TO GET YOUR TREAT!

Mandee, I remember a story that Uncle Bob told us. Uncle Bob was 12 years old and his brother, Uncle Ron, was 13. They went Trick-or-Treating together without anyone else along. They knocked on a door and said "Trick-or-Treat!" An old man answered the door and said, "What wonderful costumes you two have! Why don't you come inside my living room and show my wife. She is in a wheelchair and can't come to the door."

If something like this happens to you, "SAY NO! RUN AWAY! AND TELL A TRUSTED ADULT!" Remember, don't go into a stranger's house unless your mom or dad are with you!

Uncle Bob and Uncle Ron felt sorry for his wife, so they went inside to show her their costumes. When they entered the house, the old man shut and locked the door behind them. Uncle Bob and Uncle Ron saw that there wasn't anyone else in the living room, just the old man.

They were scared and knew they had made a big mistake by going into the house. Uncle Bob said, "HEY!, you better let us go! Our father is a policeman and he is waiting outside for us at the corner!"

The old man unlocked the door and Uncle Bob and Uncle Ron ran out the door and ran home. They were lucky to get out of the old man's house. Uncle Bob and Uncle Ron never entered another strangers house after that happened to them. Uncle Bob told us this story because he loves us and wants us to be safe.

Bobby, I remember that story and I won't enter anyone's house unless mom, dad, you, and I know them really well.

Now back to the tips. I'll make sure that we are home by 8:30 p.m. just like we promised. And I won't eat any of the treats until mom, or dad has inspected them, to make sure they are safe for me to eat.

Mandee, that was awesome the way you remembered all the safety tips for Halloween. Let's go eat dinner and then change into our costumes. We're meeting our friends at 6:00 p.m. so we can go TRICK-or-TREATING.

QUESTIONS

1. Why are makeup, and hats, safer than masks
   answer on page 2

2. What should you look for when buying a mask?
   answer on page 2

3. Why should your costume have reflective markings on it?
   answer on page 3

4. Why shouldn't you have your name, address, and phone number written on the outside of your costume?
   answer on page 3

5. Why should your costume, and everything that goes with it, be fire resistant?
   answer on page 4

6. Why shouldn't you use a paper or a cloth sack for your trick-or-treat bag?
   answer on page 4

7. If you're going to use a sword, gun, or knife for your costume, why should it look like a toy and be flexible?
   answer on page 5 b

8. Why should the costume fit and not be to long?
   answer on page 6

9. Why should you have dinner before you go Trick-or-Treating?
   answer on page 7

10. Why should you have your parents check your Trick-or-Treat candy before you eat it?

   answer on page 7

11. If you're 12 years old, or younger, who should you go Trick- or-Treating with and why?

   answer on page 7

12. If you're 13 years old, or older, at least how many friends should you be with?

   answer on page 8

13. Why should you take a cell phone with you?

   answer on page 9

14. Why should you stay in your neighborhood and follow the map that you made with your parents?

   answer on page 9

15. Why is it important to have new batteries in your flashlight for tonight?

   answer on page 10

16. If your costume, or a friends costume, catches on fire, what should you do?

   answer on page 11

17. Why is it important to walk on the sidewalk or the farthest edge of the street?

   answer on page 12

18. Why is it important to stay on well lit streets, and walk everywhere, when you are Trick-or-Treating?

   answer on page 12

19. Why shouldn't you crisscross a street or cross from between parked cars?
answer on page 13

20. Why should you only cross the streets at the crosswalks?
answer on page 14

21. Who should strangers in cars talk to?
answer on page 15

22. Should you wander off by yourself when you're Trick-or-Treating? Why?
answer on page 16

23. Why should you only Trick-or-treat at well lit houses?
answer on page 17

24. Why should you always say "THANK YOU" when you receive a treat?
answer on page 17

25. Should you take a treat from a person in a car? Why Not?
answer on page 18

26. Where should you always accept your treat at when you're Trick-or-Treating? Why?
answer on page 19

27. What happened to Uncle Bob and Uncle Ron?
answer on pages 21-23

28. Why should you be home at the time you and your parent agreed on?
thought question

Printed in the United States
By Bookmasters